LA HISTORIA NUMÉRICA

THE NUMBER STORY

SMALL BOOK ONE

ENGLISH - SPANISH

Numbers Teach Children
Their Number Names

written and illustrated by

MISS ANNA

Early Reader Edition of *The Number Story 1*
Bronze Medal Winner, 2016 Wishing Shelf Book Award

Copyright © 2018 by Jieeun Woo
Illustrations © Jieeun Woo

Cover by Lumpy Publishing
Layout by | Lumpy Publishing
Translated by Leticia Stalling and Anna
Coloring by Jieeun Woo and Maria Mirabella

All rights reserved. No part of this book may be reproduced or transmitted in any form or by any means whatsoever, including photocopying, recording or by any information storage and retrieval system, without written permission from the publisher and/or author: missanna@missannabooks.com.

Library of Congress Control Number: 2018902040

Names: Miss Anna, author.
Title: Number story : numbers teach children their number names / Miss Anna.
Description: Portland, OR: Lumpy Publishing, 2018.
Identifiers: ISBN 978-1-945977-23-7 | LCCN 2018902040
Summary: The pictures and rhymes present stories which introduce numbers 0-10.
Subjects: LCSH Numeration—English--Spanish--Pictorial works--Juvenile literature. | BISAC JUVENILE NONFICTION /
Languages: English--Spanish
Classification: LCC QA141.3 .M57 2018 | DDC 513—dc23

Publisher: Lumpy Publishing
Website: www.missannabooks.com
Email: missanna@missannabooks.com

Paperback: ISBN 978-1-945977-23-7
Printed in the U.S.A.   1 3 5 7 9 10 8 6 4 2

¿Quieres aprender sobre
nuestros nombres numéricos?

It is very easy and a lot of fun!

¡Es muy fácil y divertido!

Say-along our little jingle

Cantenlo con nuestro pequeño *jingle*

starting from Number One!

a partir del Número Uno!

1

ONE   looks like my one finger.

UNO

se parece a un dedo.

ONE!
¡UNO!

2
TWO   trails a tail.
DOS
menea la cola.

A TAIL! ¡UNA COLA!

3

THREE has bumps.

TRES

tiene las curvas.

BUMPY! ¡LAS CURVAS!

4

4
A SAIL!
¡UNA VELA!

5
FIVE   is a racing track.

CINCO

es una pista de carreras.

VROOM
¡BRUM!

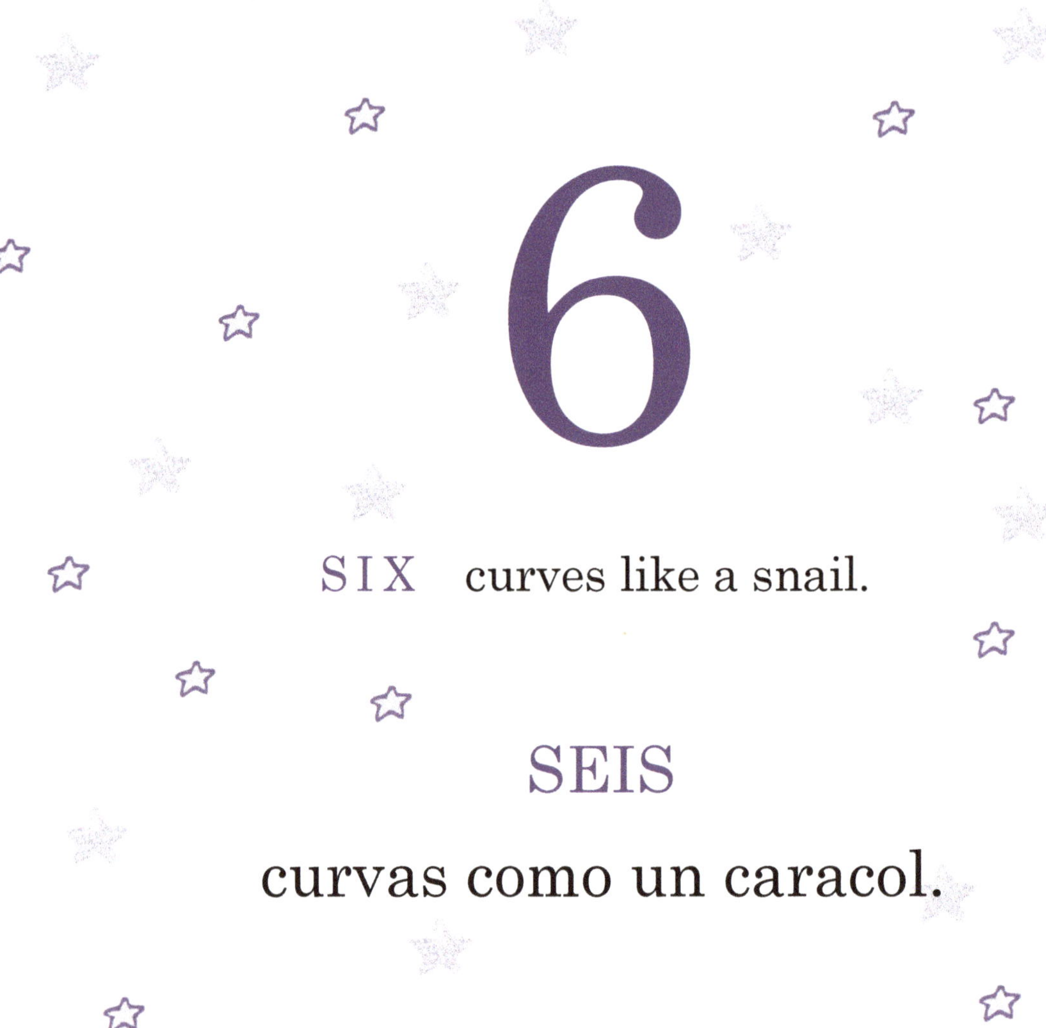

6

SIX curves like a snail.

SEIS

curvas como un caracol.

A SNAIL! ¡UN CARACOL!

7

 has a sharp angle.

SIETE

tiene un ángulo afilado.

OUCH!
¡AUCH!

8

EIGHT is rollercoaster rails.

OCHO

es una montaña rusa.

¡YUPIIII!
YIPPEE!

9

NINE   is a bubble on a stick.

NUEVE

es una burbuja en un palo.

A BUBBLE! ¡UNA BURBUJA!

10

TEN is an eye of a whale.

DIEZ

es el ojo de una ballena.

WINK!
¡Guiño!

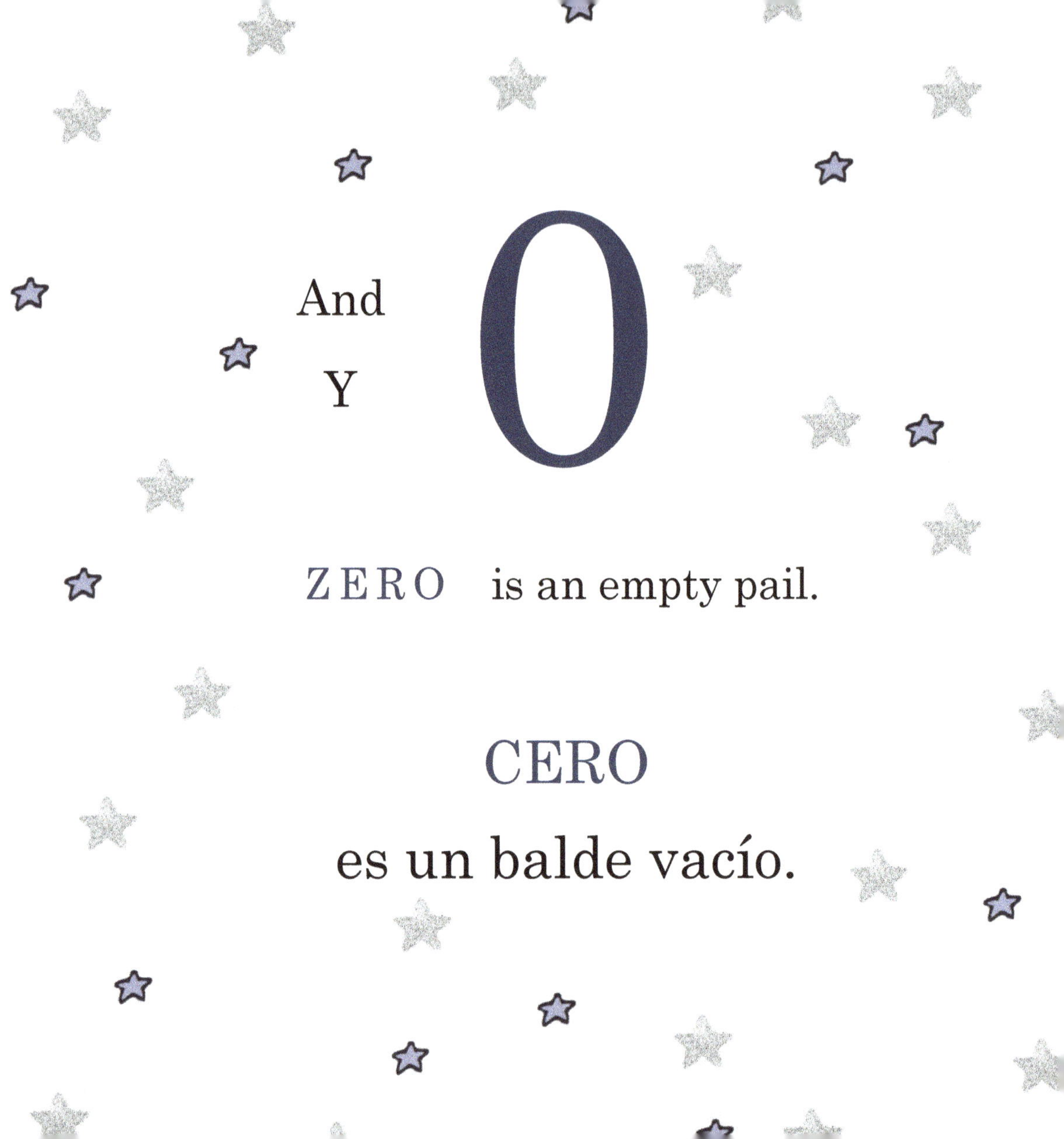

And
Y

0

ZERO   is an empty pail.

CERO

es un balde vacío.

IT'S
EMPTY!
¡Está vacío!

Thank you for playing with us today.

We had a lot of fun too!

Gracias por jugar con nosotros hoy.

¡También nos divertimos mucho!

We are your Number friends,
Zero to Ten,
Who will be here for you~
Somos tus Número-amigos
de Cero a Diez
que estarán aquí para ti~

Bye-bye now!
See you again soon!
¡Hasta luego!
¡Nos vemos pronto!

The Numbers are *SINGING* too!

To sing-a-long, look for Miss Anna Number Story
at your favorite music store like iTUNES.

MP3

Numbers 0-10
IDENTIFYING
& COUNTING

Numbers 11-20
& Ordinals
first, second, third...

Numbers 0-100
& Place Values
ones, tens, hundreds...

About Clocks
& Telling Time
hours, minutes, seconds

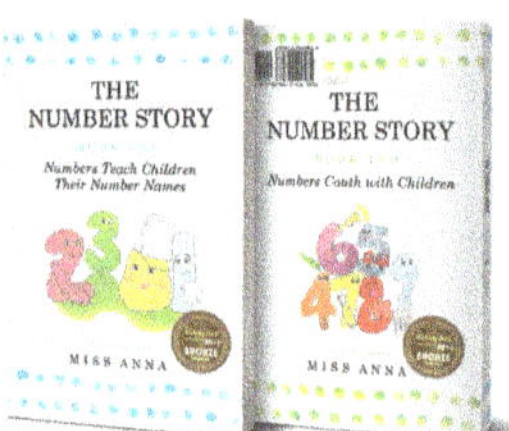

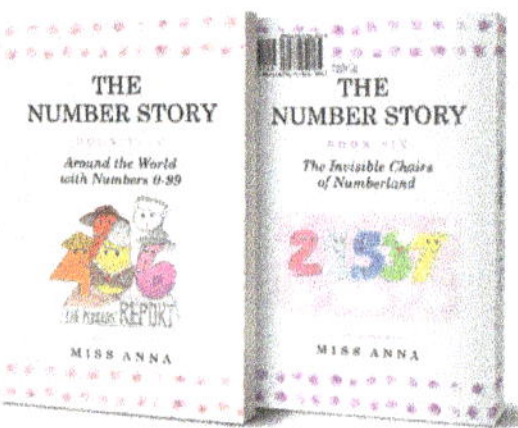
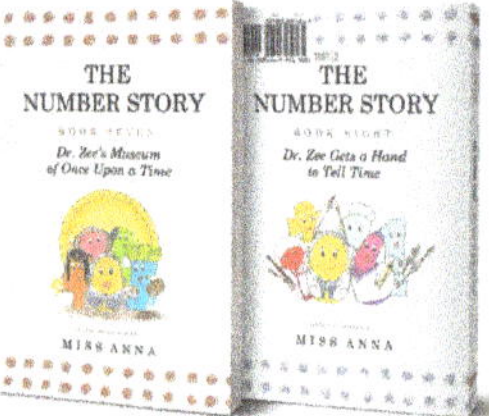

Number Story 1 & 2
isbn: 978-0-996216-48-7

Number Story 3 & 4
isbn: 978-1-945977-01-5

Number Story 5 & 6
isbn: 978-1-945977-06-0

Number Story 7 & 8
isbn: 978-1-949320-40-4

For more Miss Anna books to love,
visit us at

www.missannabooks.com

Numbers are working hard all over the world!
Come Travel the World with Us!

www.ingramcontent.com/pod-product-compliance
Lightning Source LLC
Chambersburg PA
CBHW041100050726
47599CB00018B/2220